Anna Mika

The Importance of Codes of Ethics
Examination of the Need of Business Ethics and the Efficient Usage of Codes of Ethics for Good Corporate Governance

**Bachelor + Master
Publishing**

Mika, Anna: The Importance of Codes of Ethics: Examination of the Need of Business Ethics and the Efficient Usage of Codes of Ethics for Good Corporate Governance, Hamburg, Diplomica Verlag GmbH 2011
Originaltitel der Abschlussarbeit: The Importance of Codes of Ethics: Examination of the Need of Business Ethics and the Efficient Usage of Codes of Ethics for Good Corporate Governance

ISBN: 978-3-86341-116-9
Druck: Bachelor + Master Publishing, ein Imprint der Diplomica® Verlag GmbH, Hamburg, 2011
Zugl. Hochschule für Technik und Wirtschaft Berlin, Berlin, Deutschland, Masterarbeit, 2010

Bibliografische Information der Deutschen Nationalbibliothek:
Die Deutsche Nationalbibliothek verzeichnet diese Publikation in der Deutschen Nationalbibliografie;
detaillierte bibliografische Daten sind im Internet über http://dnb.d-nb.de abrufbar.

Die digitale Ausgabe (eBook-Ausgabe) dieses Titels trägt die ISBN 978-3-86341-616-4 und kann über den Handel oder den Verlag bezogen werden.

Dieses Werk ist urheberrechtlich geschützt. Die dadurch begründeten Rechte, insbesondere die der Übersetzung, des Nachdrucks, des Vortrags, der Entnahme von Abbildungen und Tabellen, der Funksendung, der Mikroverfilmung oder der Vervielfältigung auf anderen Wegen und der Speicherung in Datenverarbeitungsanlagen, bleiben, auch bei nur auszugsweiser Verwertung, vorbehalten. Eine Vervielfältigung dieses Werkes oder von Teilen dieses Werkes ist auch im Einzelfall nur in den Grenzen der gesetzlichen Bestimmungen des Urheberrechtsgesetzes der Bundesrepublik Deutschland in der jeweils geltenden Fassung zulässig. Sie ist grundsätzlich vergütungspflichtig. Zuwiderhandlungen unterliegen den Strafbestimmungen des Urheberrechtes.

Die Wiedergabe von Gebrauchsnamen, Handelsnamen, Warenbezeichnungen usw. in diesem Werk berechtigt auch ohne besondere Kennzeichnung nicht zu der Annahme, dass solche Namen im Sinne der Warenzeichen- und Markenschutz-Gesetzgebung als frei zu betrachten wären und daher von jedermann benutzt werden dürften.

Die Informationen in diesem Werk wurden mit Sorgfalt erarbeitet. Dennoch können Fehler nicht vollständig ausgeschlossen werden, und die Diplomarbeiten Agentur, die Autoren oder Übersetzer übernehmen keine juristische Verantwortung oder irgendeine Haftung für evtl. verbliebene fehlerhafte Angaben und deren Folgen.

© Bachelor + Master Publishing, ein Imprint der Diplomica® Verlag GmbH
http://www.diplom.de, Hamburg 2011
Printed in Germany

Abbreviations

CC	-	Corporate Citizenship
CG	-	Corporate Governance
CR	-	Corporate Responsibility
CRI	-	Corporate Responsibility Index
CSR	-	Corporate Social Responsibility
EU	-	European Union
FDI	-	Foreign Direct Investment
GATT	-	General Agreement on Tariffs and Trade
GCCG	-	German Code of Corporate Governance
ICC	-	International Chamber of Commerce
ILO	-	International Labour Office
MNE	-	Multinational Enterprise
NATO	-	North Atlantic Treaty Organisation
NGO	-	Non-governmental Organisation
OECD	-	Organisation of Economic Cooperation and Development
UN	-	United Nations
SOA	-	Sarbanes-Oxley act
SRI	-	Social Responsible Investing
WTO	-	World Trade Organisation

Table of Content

I. Introduction 9
   I.1 Motivation 9
   I.2 Issues 9
   I.3 Structure 10

II. Business ethics and codes of ethics 13
   II.1 The philosophy of ethics 13
   II.2 The evolution of business ethics 15
   II. 3 History of business ethics 15
   II. 4 Business ethics and codes of ethics 17
   II. 5 Business ethics and its forms and definitions 18
   II.6 Business ethics and globalisation 20

III. Examination of the need of business ethics and the efficient usage of codes of ethics 23
   III. 1 Hypothesis I: There is a need for business ethics 23
      III. 1.1 Evidence in reference to philosophy 23
      III.1.2 Evidence in reference to Adam Smith and modern capitalism 24
      III.1.3 Evidence in reference to the industrialisation 26
      III.1.4 Evidence in reference to the principal-agent-theory and opportunistic behaviour 26
      III.1.5 Evidence in reference to the globalisation and increase of MNEs 29
      III.1.6 Evidence in reference to cultural and legislative influence 30
      III.1.7 Evidence in reference to customer power 32
      III.1.8 Evidence by reference in to public media and NGOs 33
      III.1.9 Critique on business ethics 34
      III.1.10 Economical and reputational gain of business ethics 36
      III.1.11 Measurement of impact of business ethics 37
      III.1.12 Conclusion of hypothesis I 38
   III.2 Hypothesis II: The efficient usage of codes of ethics can improve corporate governance 39
      III.2.1 Definition and development of codes of ethics 40
      III.2.2 Various types of codes of ethics 41
      III.2.3 Motives for the implementation of codes of ethics 42
      III.2.4 Implementation and effectiveness of codes of ethics 43

    III.2.5 Gain Mehrwert of codes of ethics 46

    III.2.6 Critique on codes of ethics 48

    III.2.7 Future outlook for codes of ethics 48

    III.2.8 Conclusion for hypothesis II 49

IV. Conclusion 51

V. References 53

I. Introduction

I.1 Motivation

During my time of studying business and economy, I have been fascinated by the fact that nearly everything in our world is influenced by the global economy. Every simple trade transaction or exchange of services involves a lot of people and impacts several countries nowadays. The constant rise of the globalisation produced multinational enterprises with a lot of power and control over big parts of the world's resources. The decay of human moral understanding and the recent scandals due to unethical business practices promoted my interest of multicultural and ethical business. The change in the business ethos and the grey zones emerged due to country differences supported unethical business behaviour. Ethics and moral as defined thousands of years ago by the first philosophers need to be taken seriously again. Especially, by institutions, which have an influence on many people and our environment, as businesses have nowadays. My goal is to illustrate this importance of business ethics and their main instrument, the codes of ethics.

I.2 Issues

Is there really a need for business ethics? If everybody would act morally, why is then everybody talking about ethics in the business context?

Following the thoughts of Aristotle's virtue ethics and Kant's categorical imperative, there would be no need of business ethics since everybody would be trustworthy and respect the society and the nature. Recent scandals on the other hand illustrated that ethics and moral are not well-known in enterprises with its main goal of profit maximization and that managers tend to live against the categorical imperative. The debate about the connection between business and ethics started with the birth of modern capitalism and intensified with the industrialisation and globalisation. Capitalistic thoughts, increase of corporations and individualization of humans created opportunistic behaviour, which is incompatible with the moral of values according to Aristotle. The globalization and impact of growing number of stakeholders aggravate the situation of the society's moral understanding. Through NGOs and media pressure and a change in customer's attitudes towards corporate responsibilities the awareness of a missing moral occurred. Multinational enterprises have to face various dilemmas caused by differences in cultures and national laws. These diversities and gaps on the global level provoke grey zones, which corporations can take and some already took advantage of. To face the challenges of uncontrolled managerial misbehaviour, codes of ethics as moral guiding principles can be very useful and some manager started to realize the advantages. The voluntary codes of ethics can be a guideline for managers, employees and even suppliers. Also, it gives the company an encouragement of the corporate identity and vision, which leads to motivation and cooperation. In this paper, the importance of ethics in business and codes of ethics will be shown in the context of the changing economic world and the codes' positive impacts on Corporate Governance, if the ethical guidelines are implemented and lived in the right manner.

I.3 Structure

The paper starts with a description of ethics and moral in a philosophical context and then passes on to the growing awareness of ethics in business. The history of business ethics gives a first overview about the significant change in the economy and the increasing need for moral in business patterns. This part of the paper also covers the corporate challenges occurring due to the globalisation and their impact on business ethics. The next section defines business ethics and its fellows, such as codes of ethics, Corporate Social Responsibility, Corporate Governance, Corporate Responsibility, Corporate Citizenship and Corporate Compliance. These fundamentals are the foundation for the two hypotheses.

The next chapter examines the two hypotheses of this thesis. The first hypothesis deals with the need for business ethics and the second hypothesis tries to evolve the importance of codes of ethics. The hypothesis about the need for business ethics is debated by several different aspects. Through falling back on the philosophy, the need is discussed with the help of Aristotle and Kant. Afterwards, the assumption, if ethics is necessary in the economy, is explored by the history of modern capitalism and Adam Smith's theories. The debate about corporate social and ethical responsibilities exists since the birth of modern capitalism and the changes due to the industrialisation. In this time, the first problems of opportunistic behaviour occurred because of the separation of ownership and control. Companies started to grow and to enlarge their business relations and practices on a global level. This fact brought along various multicultural stakeholders and a variation of interests. The differences in cultures and national laws disclosed several moral dilemmas for business people. This point of the exploration of the first hypothesis illustrates very briefly, a need for an ethical consideration in business practices. The next aim deals with the influence of consumer power on businesses and the customers' changing attitude towards more responsible enterprises. Several other sources of pressure to covering the moral idea of business practices exist. After exploring the critique, the economic gain of ethical behaviour will be illustrated and the way of measuring this. The first hypothesis will be ended by concluding the findings.

The second hypothesis examines the importance of codes of ethics and their influences on Corporate Governance. This part of the thesis begins with a definition of codes and evaluates the path of developing codes. The differences in codes of ethics will be explained and some examples will be named. Furthermore, the right implementation of codes will be illustrated in detail as that is the prerequisite of a code to be effective. The proper implementation and the effectiveness of codes of ethics are then assumed to assess the influence of codes and their economical gain. After naming some critics and a future outlook, the second hypothesis will be concluded.

At the end of the paper, in the fourth chapter, the findings will be completed and the importance of ethics in business and codes of ethics will be illustrated.

The thesis is based on secondary literature published between the 1970s and 2010.

II. Business ethics and codes of ethics

II.1 The philosophy of ethics

Ethics is a philosophical phenomenon, which with humans examine since several thousand years. Ethics, as a part of philosophy, deals mainly with morality. Behind the term ethics are the main issues about right and wrong behaviour in a society and a moral understanding of human beings concealed. The world of ethics includes mainly three parts, as there are applied ethics, normative ethics and metaethics. Whereas metaethics is dealing with the theoretical approach of morality, the normative ethics includes more practical issues to create moral standards in different societies. The applied ethics involves controversial situations and the moral way of acting. This part of ethics is the science of giving a moral guideline for the 'right' behaviour in troubling situations in the society and also in the business world. Accordingly, business ethics is a part of the applied ethics.[1] The study of morality is the main part of ethics and gives the basis of human behaviour based in the character. The moral of a person is based on rules, which help to live and react in the society. The value system increases the ethical behaviour and leads to principles according to the specific manner people act and which guides them in controversial cases. Human beings have the ability to think objectively about situations and their role inside these moments, to choose rational between given options and commit to their behaviour. Most of these actions are based on intuitionism and impartiality, which come from the basic moral beliefs and the inclusions of other persons due to the fact that humans are social and have the tempted need to live in a group. A part of moral fundamentals is the fact to respect the life of the persons around oneself and to treat everybody in a manner as one want to be treaded oneself.[2]

Ethics, as a science, covers the main questions about how to live the life in a good manner. The human sense for ethics is based in his moral understanding of the things happening in the world. The basis of this understanding is build due to experiences, traditions and parental teaching and forms the beliefs of people. The freedom of choice, which is given to every living creature on this planet, can lead to problematic situations, which maybe overwhelm the participants of the circumstances. This freedom of choice

---

[1] Richard. 1989. There is ethics in business ethics; but there's more as well, pp. 337-339.

[2] Newton. 2005. Business ethics and the natural environment, pp. 11-19.

can be compensated due to moral understanding of humans, which gives a guideline for proper behaviour.[3]

The ancient Greeks already argued that people who live in an amoral manner and are just self-absorbed, are mainly living against the sense of what human beings represent and are hurting themselves deep in their soul. Plato and Socrates argued in a similar manner. Although morality is subjective, it is a very important part of the existence of humans. As it is visible in the history, people debate and protest, even used and still use violent behaviour to stick to their moral beliefs. In the last thousands of years different patterns and theories of ethics have being evolved. According to the consequentiality view, the morally best action is what will bring the greatest consequences to all being influenced by this action.[4] Immanuel Kant, one of the most popular ethical theorists, explained moral and ethics by his theory of the categorical imperative. His theory is named as the basis of rational ethics and points out that all humans should arrange their own behaviour according to the welfare of the others.[5] Kant thought about moral behaviour as a set of maxims, which are created by every single person according to its moral rationality. The categorical imperative stresses out that everybody should act as the personal maxim can lead to a universal law. Kant's theory is categorical because it is absolutely tied to human moral behaviour. The imperative calls out the guiding part about how one must act. Kant always stressed out the respect for all humans and the existence of humans moral dignity. In his means, people do the right decisions for the right reasons. In corporate context, this idea has sometimes been confused and managers tended to make the right thing just for profit or image reasons. This perspective is not moral, it is more prudential. A moral action has to have a good will according to the Kantian view. Another ethical fundament is the utilitarianism. This approach claims that a good human condition is one, which brings the greatest happiness to everything that can be happy and an activity can be seen as morally right, when the good is balanced over the bad. The principle of utility commits to the principle of maximization of the net good outcome. Placed in the business perspective the utilitarianism gives the principle of the maximization of productivity through efficiency because the source of maximiza-

---

[3] Machan/Chesher. 2002. A primer on Business Ethics, pp. xiii-xv.

[4] Adams/Maine. 1998. Business ethics for the 21st century, pp. 1-13.

[5] Albach. 2005. Unternehmensethik: ein subjektiver Überblick, pp. 1-5.

tion is the efficiency. And the good and efficient organisation of a corporation leads to higher profits, which is an economic goal.[6]

II.2 The evolution of business ethics

One of the oldest connections between ethics and economics was invented by Aristotle, a Greek philosopher, in the fourth century BC. Aristotle pointed out that a life of a human being is good, if it is lived according to human nature. He meant that humans often make their life worse because they mainly think about short-term pleasure and are not aware about the long-term effects of their decisions. Aristotle was against the economical drive because he believed that everything what business behaviour represents is against the nature of human beings and 'bad' for the character. Business practices spoil the internal nature of people and show a lack of self-control.[7] According to Aristotle the 'moral virtue' gives humans the habit to make the morally right decisions. The primary purpose of morality is the development of a virtuous character. People doing business tend to miss virtues and also moral instinct. Based on Aristotle, the neo-Aristotelian perspective defines ethics as a structure of guiding principles.[8] In line with these thoughts, business ethics is an effort to create practical rules for moral business behaviour. By specifying the ethical norms and rules concrete guidelines were created. In times of Aristotle these guiding parameters were based on trust, prudence and honesty of the moral business men.[9] Nowadays, these guidelines occur under the term 'code of ethics'.

II. 3 History of business ethics

The influence, reach and importance of business ethics can be best shown by drawing the historical development of ethics and moral in the business context. Ethics is way longer a part of business as many business people may believe. In 1907, first moral guidelines for business behaviour were developed and even managers of big corporations started to claim: 'The greater the corporation, the greater its responsibility.'[10] In the 1930s, Berle and Dodd discussed the responsibilities of multinational enterprises

---

[6] Beauchamp/Bowie. 2004. Ethical theory and business, pp. 16-27.

[7] Adams/Maine. 1998. Business ethics for the 21st century, pp. 25-27.

[8] Machan/Chester. 2002. A Primer on business ethics, pp. 42-43.

[9] Beauchamp/Bowie. 2004. Ethical theory and business, pp. 28-38.

[10] Böhm. 1979. Gesellschaftliche verantwortliche Unternehmensführung, p. 53.

(MNEs) and their opinion was that big corporations are very powerful and will misuse this power, if they are not managed in the interest of the public. In the 1960s, due to the environmental decline and the Vietnam War, there was a change in consumers' position. The costumers started to realize that the superior position of corporations needs to be used for a positive change and that the MNEs needed to be more controlled. Especially due to the globalisation, the corporations started to operate all over the world and were harder to control by governmental legislation. On the flipside, claims became loud that the only responsibility of corporations is to maximize the shareholder value and that the only social act in business is to increase the profits. The most important adherent of this viewpoint was Milton Friedman. In the 1980s, a series of takeovers and acquisitions started because of the overall increase in Foreign Direct Investment (FDI) at this time. Most of these took place without any social thought or moral behaviour. The most significance change facing business ethics took place at the end of the 1990s, respectively the beginning of the twenties century and with the end of the Cold War. New technologies occurred, which led to a higher productivity worldwide, but also an improvement in communication technologies and therefore better informed consumers.[11] Another big influencer of the increasing involvement of ethics in business topics was the signing of the General Agreement on Tariffs and Trade (GATT) after World War II and the development of other important trade zones. Capitalism started to grow and became a worldwide trend.[12] In the second half of the nineteen's century, the existence of multinational and global corporations increased. This delivered alteration because the activities of such big firms, which operates in different countries, exceeded the regular economically actions. Also John D. Rockefeller mentioned factors that are importantly connected to the industry and the corporations are capital, management, labour and also the community. As one of the first, he realized that social responsibility of corporations obverse the community is just as important as profit making.[13] The 'evolution of expectations' showed that the social responsibility of MNEs is a moving target. The change in the expectations, what business is or should be all about, did not just make the consumers and non-governmental organisations sit up, but also the managers. In the course of the 70s, more and more manager started to take verbal confessions concerning the social impact their company has on the community and the

---

[11] Shestack. 2005. CSR in a changing corporate world, pp. 98-100.

[12] Adams/Maine. 1998. Business ethics for the 21st century, pp. 3-4.

[13] Böhm. 1979. Gesellschaftliche verantwortliche Unternehmensführung, p. 54.

ways to show more responsibility towards the stakeholders. During this period, the importance of ethics in business and codes of ethics got more visible than ever.[14] Due to the changes activated by globalisation and the scandals about unethical behaviour of multinational enterprises in the United States, international business ethics became more and more important.

II. 4 Business ethics and codes of ethics

The above mentioned pressure by the public is one reason for the invention of codes of ethics, but mainly a voluntary reason. In the United States, due to the scandals in the last decade, public corporations are legislatively forced to disclose a code of ethics. This development took place in 2002 and was called the Sarbanes-Oxley-Act. In the same year, the Nasdaq stock market and the New York Stock Exchange obliged the disclosure of codes of ethics for all listed companies.[15] Codes of corporate conduct exist nearly a century, but got the main attention in the 1960s and 1970s. At that time, corporations, international organisations and national governments started to invent and adopt codes of conduct. The most considerable codes in the 70s were invented by the OECD (Organisation of Economic Cooperation and Development) in 1976 and the ILO (International Labour Office) in 1977. The codes of these two organisations are the pioneers of ethical code development. They represent the basis for most of the individual corporate codes, which development exploited in the 1980s. The origin of codes of ethics and the first formal code ever was authored in 1937 by the International Chamber of Commerce (ICC). These standards were invented to eliminate competition between the ICC members and to avoid the damage of the environment and society in the member countries.[16] According to the ILO, analysts acknowledged four different types of generations of issues in codes. The content of the first generation is dealing with the conflict of interest and is more focused on the interests of the corporation. The second, third and fourth generations are concerning with the public interests and are based on the commercial conduct, the rights of the employees and the rights of the human and the community. The corporate codes of ethics are respectively a part of the first genera-

---

[14] Ibid, p. 11.
[15] Schwartz. 2004. Effective Corporate Codes of ethics: Perceptions of Code Users, pp. 323–343.
[16] Mamic. 2004. Implementing codes of conduct, pp. 36-37.

tion.[17] Modern codes are mainly based on these pioneers and are various due to different industries and the differences based in the corporation's nature.

II. 5 Business ethics and its forms and definitions

Codes are a part of the movement of the last century towards business ethics. Based on this development, terms as Corporate Social Responsibility (CSR), Corporate Governance, Corporate Responsibility (CR), Corporate Citizenship (CC) and the compliance of the corporation were created. They all deal with ethics and morality in business patterns. This development is mainly based on a new understanding of business relationships towards the employees, the community and the environment. In the last decades, some companies started to think about the interests of their stakeholder and tried to increase the overall economical welfare. Also several managers started to promote their support of social issues and their role of good Corporate Citizens.[18]

Business ethics, as the generic term, has itself no clear definition. It is rather the other way around. The existence of too many different definitions of business ethics can cause confusion. In business terms, business ethics is a mixture of moral principles connected to daily business behaviour and its impact on the stakeholders and the community involved.[19] According to another author, business ethics combines values, Corporate Governance and codes of ethics. Business ethics has its focus more on morality at which Corporate Social Responsibility (CSR) spotlights the social, sustainable and environmental issues of business.[20]

The rising tendency towards Corporate Social Responsibility is a mirror of the change in modern business. The reality of daily business shows that business and society are interwoven and that the expectations on both sides changed. Corporations realize the impact of the society and change their attitude towards it. The society on the other hand expects nowadays more from a company as to make profits. The pyramid of CSR reflects this point of view. The basis of the pyramid with its economic and legal responsibilities meets the requirements of a corporation. The top of the pyramid, which includes the ethically and philanthropy responsibilities get more in the focus at the

---

[17] International Labour Office. 2001. Codes of conduct and multinational enterprises, chapter I.

[18] Böhm. 1979. Gesellschaftliche verantwortliche Unternehmensführung, p. 10.

[19] http://www.allbusiness.com/glossaries/business-ethics/4962856-1.html

[20] Thomas. 2005. Business ethics, pp. 31-36.

present time. Especially the crisis, due to corporate scandals, underlines the significance of CSR all along with Corporate Governance.[21]

The social responsibility of corporations and the Corporate Governance have some parts in common. But more interestingly is their main significant difference. CSR is voluntary and based on ethical rules, whereas Corporate Governance is mainly a binding law.[22] In the United States of America is the Corporate Governance statue and policy based since the introduction of the Sarbanes-Oxley-Act (SOA) in 2002. In Europe, the governance of corporations is to some parts still a voluntary soft law. Corporate Governance is defined by the OECD as a system to control corporations and the accountability enterprises have towards all their stakeholders.[23] Based on that context and the increase in complexity in the globalized world, it would make sense to ensure Corporate Governance as a binding law on a global scale. One example for the contrary of the SOA is the German Code of Corporate Governance (GCCG), which was invented in 2000 and represents a guideline for the management and control of German corporations.[24]

As mentioned above, there are several different terms combined under the generic term business ethics. Next to CSR and Corporate Governance, there are also terms which define different issues of ethics in business. Corporate Responsibility (CR) for example is a part of Corporate Social Responsibility. This branch deals mainly with the interests of the stakeholders. The issue of profit maximization as the only corporate goal and the responsibilities towards the community and the environment are of main importance in this field. Corporate Responsibility also comprises parts of Corporate Governance and Corporate Citizenship.[25]

Corporate Citizenship spells out the way, in which a company means to act in a community as a good citizen. Corporations commit to behave as one of the neighbourhood and not just to offer workplaces, but also to give support within the area and its environmental system.[26]

---

[21] Luo. 2007. Global dimensions of corporate governance, pp. 197-199.

[22] Mullerat. 2005. The global responsibility of business, pp. 3-5.

[23] Walsh/Cowry. 2005. CSR and corporate governance, pp. 38-53.

[24] Pfitzer/Oser. 2003. Deutscher Corporate Governance Kodex, pp. VI-VII.

[25] http://www.business-ethics.org/primer.asp

[26] Schmeisser, et al. 2009. Shareholder Value approach versus Social Responsibility, pp. 85-88.

Corporate Compliance gives a guideline of regulations and rules for employees and managers. The invention of Corporate Compliance and in some companies even a compliance manager, was mainly done to defend the enterprise against violating behaviour of managers and employees and for this reason arising expensive lawsuits. The innovation of Corporate Compliance started in the 1980s in relation to the first big corporation scandals.[27]

II.6 Business ethics and globalisation

Business ethics on an international level faces way more challenges as bringing ethical behaviour in country-specific business transactions. Multinational enterprises have to face the differences in cultures and due to that the different traditions and also various religions, which all influence the moral understanding and per se the behaviour of the people. These differences can lead to controversial opinions of ethically 'right' behaviour.[28]

The increase in advertence in business ethics was mainly dependent on the challenges the globalisation brought along. In the last century, barriers of trade were removed and the worldwide production, flow of trade and capital increased and more and more strategically alliances were adopted. Due to this development, a maceration of national borders occurred and the denationalisation started to grow. The invention of the North Atlantic Treaty Organisation (NATO) and the European Union (EU) are good examples for that shift of geographical and also political borders.[29] That led among other things to legislative problems. It was generated a deferral of the competency and differences in the laws around the globe. That fact gave the multinational enterprises the opportunity to use the outcome of this, namely the grey zones for amoral profit maximisation. It is not everything illegal worldwide, what is seen as unethical. These facts brought up critique concerning globalisation. Reviewers argue that the principles of globalisation with its protection for free trade and an open marketplace are not appropriate for less developed countries and leaves too much room for corporations to profit from the non-industrial countries.[30] Although these critiques, Peter Senge is talking about a revolution, which happens right now caused by the globalisation. He mentions that an interre-

---

[27] Geißler. 2004. Was ist compliance management?

[28] Karmasin/Litschka. 2008. Wirtschaftsethik – Theorien, Strategien, pp. 176-182.

[29] Beisheim, et al. 1999. Im Zeitalter der Globalisierung? pp. 16, 266-320.

[30] Machan/Chester. 2002. A Primer on business ethics, pp. 159-169.

lation exists due to the disappearance of the national boarders and that it is dependent on business and non-business organisations to realize that the whole world is interconnected. Humans tend to think in a moral manner, but also tend to act not that way as are corporations and their managers. The global businesses have nowadays the chance to change something and close the grey zones by acting ethical.[31] Non-governmental organisations (NGOs) have an increasing awareness of this 'greenwashing' of corporations' image and started to make such behaviour public. Even though, multinational enterprises invented social responsibility programs, the amoral behaviour for seeking profit did not stop eventually. Nowadays, corporations are mainly forced to behave in the right manner due to the invention and interconnection of the globalisation. New technologies in the communication area give the consumer the opportunity to inform themselves about companies and their habits before purchasing. Also non-governmental organisations invented websites, which offers facts and news about the real social behaviour of MNEs.[32]

In conclusion of this chapter, the change in the economic and business world in the last centuries was recognizable and the impacts theses changes had on the ethical attitude towards business. The main fundamentals concerning ethics, morality, the change through globalisation and the developed subjects referred to business ethics were explained. They represent a basis for the following controversy about the need of ethics in business and their main instrument the codes of ethics.

---

[31] Senge, et al. 2010. The necessary revolution, pp. 5-22.
[32] Spitzeck. 2008. Moralische Organisationsentwicklung.

III. Examination of the need of business ethics and the efficient usage of codes of ethics

The second chapter gave an overview of ethics and its forms and perspectives. Furthermore, it showed the history of ethics in business relation. The ethical understanding of morality and the context of ethics in business show the implications of business ethics. This fundamental impression will be the basis for the further two hypothesis. To call out the importance of codes of ethics in this paper, the first hypothesis will deal with business ethics and its need in the modern business world. It can be assumed that codes of ethics just can be important or effective in any way, when there is a basic need of ethics in nowadays business. To illustrate the significance of the codes, the importance of business ethics and its increasing awareness has to be referred. By means of the mentioned fundamentals as the change in the world economy due to globalization and the condition and goals of the present business world, the need for business ethics will be proofed. The second hypothesis will examine the importance of codes of ethics in the business context. This hypothesis will be analysed by firstly defining codes of ethics and investigate their development and various types. Subsequently, the reasons for adopting a code and its implementation will be discussed. This is essential due to the fact that codes just can be effective when they are implemented into the organisation and lived by all stakeholders. The effectiveness is an important requirement to analyse the importance and influence of codes of ethics. This impact of codes, as a part of an ethical organisation, will be illustrated.

III. 1 Hypothesis I: There is a need for business ethics

III. 1.1 Evidence in reference to philosophy

There are several ways to proof the need of business ethics in modern economic times. Historically, Aristotle once started the discussion about the morality of economical relations. He claimed that economic transactions harm the moral and soul of a human being. People should live according to the nature. Aristotle was against the business interactions between men because he thought that people who see money as its ends and not just as the means to buy products to fulfil the basic needs cannot have a moral meaning.[33] Immanuel Kant also saw the human happiness not in the existence of money or profit, but in the nature of people's social relationships. He argued in his categorical imperative that everybody's moral understanding and behaviour should lead in maxims, which could represent a law.[34]

---

[33] Adams/Maine. 1998. Business ethics for the 21st century, pp. 25-27.
[34] Beauchamp/Bowie. 2004. Ethical theory and business, pp. 22-27.

According to the Kantian view, all human beings should act in a morally right manner, respect the other individuals and the nature and would never harm anybody or anything to increase its own welfare. But in today's reality, there are other situations to observe, also in the world of business. Kant argued that such kind of unreasonable and insensible behaviour could be prevented, if organisations and their activities are created in such a way that the categorical imperative is not harmed.[35] Are these corporate scandals and the damaging of the environment by corporations in the last decades due to unethical behaviour a lack of morality in today's business? When did some business people start to live against the categorical imperative? Is this amoral behaviour based on the impacts of modern capitalism or does the moral structure of our society break up into itself?

If we assume that business is a respectable profession and that the people doing business follow the Kantian view, there would be no need for ethics in business. Though, there is an increase in the attention of business ethics and a creation of new terminology and even new professions surrounding the ethical impact in business practices. This fact illustrates that there is a lack of morality in business and that some people do not behave in the right and legal manner. According to the neo-Aristotelian perspective, ethics can face these dilemmas of amoral behaviour and be used as a guide of life-improving principles, no matter if these were used for the life in human society or in business relations.[36]

But as there is no 'golden rule' of ethical interpretation and due to the fact that humans are not unfailing, situations of amoral behaviour can occur. As demonstrated in history a small unethical action can sometimes be linked with enormous effects due to corporations influence on a lot of stakeholders and the environment. Because of these misconceptions, human beings tend to develop rules as norms, values and traditions to live together in a harmonious and ethical manner. These systems of guiding principles can also be very effective in corporations.[37]

III.1.2 Evidence in reference to Adam Smith and modern capitalism

By means of these various approaches and viewpoints the debate about business ethics seems meaningful. Since thousands of years, the morality and the economics were

---

[35] Albach. 2005. Unternehmensethik: ein subjektiver Überblick, pp. 8-11.

[36] Machan/Chester. 2002. A Primer on business ethics, pp. 41-42.

[37] Koch. 2008. Wirtschaftethik.

discussed and since more than hundred years now, the debate got louder and the impact of corporations and their involved responsibilities became a controversial topic. The dispute about the responsibilities of corporations rolls since the initiation of modern capitalism.[38]

To address the change in ethical understanding according business and the need of morality originated from the history of economics and modern capitalism, the story of modern economics has to be structured. The need for ethics in business cannot just be found in the depth of philosophical theories, but also in the models and realizations of economists.

In 1776, the story of modern economics started with the publication of the "Wealth of Nations" by Adam Smith. He promised in his paper economic independence and a new world, in which every working man would be free and would share the wealth of the Nations. According to his theory, the freedom in trade would increase through open borders and free movement of goods. In his belief, the system would organize itself and through a good legal system and morally distinctive businessmen, everybody would benefit and the economy would grow. Smith was confident that humans, who have the freedom to act in their interests, would create a positive result. Smith called this faith in the self-regulation of the economy the 'invisible hand'. But exactly this freedom led to damage of the environment, social trouble and the mistreatment of power. The concept of the 'invisible hand' is only working, if business men recognize the importance of long-term goals and put value-based business behaviour over the own interests. The golden rule of helping yourself by lending a hand to others is not withstanding, if the self-interest of businessmen succeed over their moral understanding.[39]

By applying Smith' theory to basic business transactions, his thoughts seem reasonable. The corporation is helping the consumer by producing goods for the human needs and the customer is dependent on the company producing these products for the daily life. But this concept does not promise that the corporations are fulfilling their tasks in an ethical manner. The liberal hope that the market is producing the public welfare through the invisible hand did not meet. Corporations were invented to serve the society and not to harm the people and the environment. The idea of wealth for everybody can be

---

[38] Adams/Maine. 1998. Business ethics for the 21st century, p. 2.
[39] Skousen. 2007. The big three in economics, pp. 3-30.

fulfilled, if companies can handle the balance between the economical and social claims. The liberal market theory and freedom of trade, as Smith declared, is regulating the market, but does not deal with the moral understanding of managers or with the challenges the industrialisation brought along.[40] This approach illustrates a need for ethical impacts in the modern economy.

III.1.3 Evidence in reference to the industrialisation

As mentioned before in Chapter II, people always tended to live in a group and are used to act according to the group, which is mainly the family or close friends. In the past, the role of this social net was essential for most of the people as they were taken care of themselves within a small community or by owning their own farm or family business. The industrialization and the capitalism brought the single person more in focus and people started to move to cities and to live without their families. This change in the social neuter of most of humans living in industrialized countries led to a decay of values and the increase of the interests of the individual. As every revolution is bringing change, the industrialisation brought wealth for the simple workingmen and new opportunities, but also problems. In the industrialized countries, there was an increase in business and growing corporations recorded. While the size of most corporations increased, it became complicated to control the organisation of such firms. With the ongoing industrialisation, new challenges occurred for the owners of big companies in the beginning of the nineteen century.[41]

III.1.4 Evidence in reference to the principal-agent-theory and opportunism

The growing complexity of the organisations made the owners hiring managers to deal with the administrative and supervisory functions. This separation of ownership and control led to new problems. It is not secured that a manager is making decisions in the interests of the owner, especially in big companies. This problem of self-interested managers realized Adam Smith already centuries ago and was later named opportunistic behaviour. This conduct of managers can lead to corporate costs. The principal-agent-theory tries to cut down this expenditure based on the separation of control and ownership. The theory implies that the principal is delegating the work to the agent and he has to complete the managing job. But this model also faces two main problems. Although

---

[40] Koch. 2008. Wirtschaftsethik.

[41] Luo. 2007. Global dimensions of corporate Governance, p. 2.

the opportunistic behaviour is tried to be minimized, the goals of the agent and the principal may differ and the supervision of the agent is not that easy task for the principals. The second disagreement between the owners and the manager can occur due to a difference in the attitude towards risk. This deviation of opinions can again lead to opportunism. As opportunistic behaviour of managers can cause negative effects for the principals and the reputation of the company, the owners create controlling systems. Corporate Governance is one method to deal with opportunism.[42] The agent-principal-model mainly favours the interests of the owners and therefore considers especially the profit maximization. The interests of the others, like the employees or the society, are disregard. According to the model, these interests are protected by the legislation. This train of thought lacks creditability due to the fact that corporations have a main influence towards their stakeholders and environment. Besides the lack of corporation's consideration about the others, the problems occurring from differences in national laws have to be added. In many countries, especially in less developed regions, the legislation is not protecting the human rights and environmental laws in a proper manner. Acting based on the principal-agent-model managers with the single goal of profit maximization can use these differences for their own purpose disregarding the society and nature surrounding them. This model is mainly criticised because of the conflicts arising out of different economic drive and moreover moral preferences of the agents and principals.[43] In most of the cases in today's reality managers were asked to lead their company in harmony with their environment, but they cannot fulfil this task because they mainly feel forced to generate the highest possible profit. In the last decades, a misuse of managerial power could be observed. The scandals in American corporations in the last years were mainly based on amoral managerial behaviour conducted by greed for money and power. These gaps in the principal-agent-theory causes harm of the ethical basics of the society and illustrate the need for more ethics in business practices. Next to Corporate Governance the implementation of ethics in business can minimize this opportunistic behaviour.

This kind of opportunism generally occurs when the agent is putting his own interest over the interests of the society. Leaving the social interests aside, is much alike leaving the moral path of life according to the referred philosophical theories. In economical

---

[42] Ibid, p. 3.

[43] Adams/Maine. 1998. Business ethics for the 21st century, pp. 31-34.

approval, these antisocial preferences are not included in the function of profit gaining. The opportunistically profit maximization of managers and ethical believes are running into each other. Managers, who are just focusing on profits without dealing with social issues, will lose their morality and this situation will affect the corporation. But managers can have a digressed moral understanding, so that they do not see their responsibility.[44]

Gaps are created by moral differences and the separation of ownership and control. To minimize the negative impacts of these gaps, an ethical approach for corporations and their managers need to be implemented as a basis of the corporation's ethical path. Because of the separation of decision and ownership it is unclear, who is responsible. It is somehow the agent as he is managing the company and is making the decisions, but generally it is the principal as he is the owner of the organisation.

The separation of control and ownership and the resulting problems which opens the path for opportunism has negative effects on social and environmental patterns. Agents are in the position to manage companies in the interest of shareholders and stakeholders, but are not always willing to do so. Philosophies argue that managers who act without being responsible will turn their selves outside the society. This leads to a new difficulty. Some business people argue about the ethical responsibilities of enterprises, facing the question, if a company can have morality. This debate has many levels, but as a corporation is not a living being, the morality of a business lies in its principals, managers and employees.[45]

The complexity of a corporation and the differences in its human execution face the challenge of finding a basic line of action and understanding. This guideline can be built on an ethical framework implemented in the corporate vision and contents of social responsibilities contents of an enterprise.

The neo-liberal economic theory of Adam Smith and the difficulties, which occurred due to the separation of control and ownership, present the missing part of ethics in modern capitalism. Business ethics is not an alternative to the modern capitalism. It is

---

[44] Albach. 2005. Unternehmensethik: ein subjektiver Überblick, pp. 9-15.
[45] Shaw. 1996. Business ethics, pp. 164-172.

more an alternative within the modern economy, which helps guiding the challenges of corporations in a fast changing globalized world.[46]

III.1.5 Evidence in reference to the globalisation and increase of MNEs

The changing attitude towards business ethics in the last decades was highly influenced by the globalisation. The decrease of trade barriers and increase of tariff agreements brought a maceration of country borders. Multinational enterprises were originated as the production, trade and consuming processes became global. As stated in Chapter II, this revolution in the world economy also created challenges for business people.

The global capitalism faced the managers with a global competition. The competitive pressure leads them to further unusual paths of doing business. A lot of corporations started to produce in other countries, mainly less developed countries to gain from the softer laws and regulations covering human and environmental rights. Moreover enterprises grew by acquiring or even unfriendly taking over other firms and then cutting employees in the emerged corporation. Managers were seduced to misuse their power to be profitable in the global game. This power of corporations increased in the last decades.[47] The 100 biggest global operating enterprises generate 10% of the worldwide GDP. Multinational enterprises nowadays have a significant influence on the world's resource capacity, environmental issues and global politics. This influence is not always misleading. MNEs also generate wealth in developing countries by producing in these countries and leaving relevant information. Furthermore, these corporations are leaving their taxes in the producing countries.[48] Corporations, which operate worldwide and are facing different cultures and legislatives, cannot be managed according to economical traditions. The growing number of stakeholders, their raising interests and the difficulties resulting out of the differences in culture and traditions illustrate the need for business ethics and its instruments as Corporate Social Responsibility.[49]

---

[46] Arns. 2008. Tue Gutes und profitiere davon, pp. 10-13.

[47] Crane/Matten. 2004. Business ethics: a European perspective, pp. 14-17.

[48] Jones/Pollitt/Bek. 2007. Multinationals in their communities, pp. 2-3.

[49] Arns. 2008. Tue Gutes und profitiere davon, pp. 10-13.

III.1.6 Evidence in reference to cultural and legislative influence

Cultural and legislative challenges always existed for corporations as soon as they left their own region. Most of the differences increase with the growing operational level of a company and are therefore described here in a global context. Corporations operating worldwide are facing stakeholders, like employees and customers with many different cultural backgrounds and also various value classifications. These differences can lead to profit maximizing advantages for enterprises by abusing softer laws of developing countries or different opinions concerning child labour. Businesses facing such kind of situations should step away from a cultural approach and define an ethical relativism. Cultural values can differ and only because it seems normal in some regions of the world that children have to work, responsible corporations should not take advantage of this difference in the value systems. This kind of dilemmas can also occur due to different national regimes and their linked differences in the legislative. The merely contempt of human rights in some countries, does not allow multinational enterprises to misuse this fact. A basis of ethical principles can be very helpful in the context of international business and guide corporations and their managers on the global level. An ethical framework also has other advantages. In debates of cultural differences in the global business context, multinational enterprises often tend to see their culture as the 'right' culture. This view lacks credibility as cultures are formed within thousands of years and cannot be assessed as 'right' or 'wrong'. Everybody who wants its own culture tolerated has to respect the other culture. Corporations, which reach different cultures and their values, have to try to respect their stakeholders various value systems and to include them into a corporate ethical framework. Multinational enterprises, which are acting ethical responsible and consider regional and cultural values of the countries, in which they operate, minimize the self-interest and maximize everybody's involved wealth.[50]

Business ethics can give a guideline for employees and managers to face the cultural differences and gives a company a moral firmness. By applying these ethical rules in the corporation, the grey zones the globalisation is offering, can be painted white. Besides, the globalisation led to more attention for CSR.[51] The denationalisation brought along international trade and production. Corporate operations do not always happen in the

---

[50] DesJardins. 2009. An introduction to Business ethics, pp. 266-268.

[51] Shestack. 2005. CSR in a changing corporate world, pp. 108-109.

home country anymore. The distance leads to a different thinking and action. Due to that fact, the environmental problems abroad and the effects of unethical behaviour are taken less into consideration. This sight of global business leads to social, sustainable, environmental, and even political dilemmas.[52]

The fact that there does not exist international values, which can be applied across different cultures, proofs the need for basic ethical assumptions, which lead the behaviour of corporations and the people operating in the name of them. The minimalist method, means making business according to the minimal basic rights by obeying the law, does not seem sufficient. The increase of influence worldwide and the contact to so many different stakeholders demand more responsibilities of corporations. In the last decades, different approaches of ethical frameworks were invented by institutions as the United Nations (UN) and the World Trade Organisation (WTO). The globalisation brought the integration of international economies and a shift from political interrelations on governmental level to global business relations. Through economic cooperation, advocates believe that poverty and the possibility of wars can be reduced. However, globalisation is giving multinational corporations the chance to harm the environment and the poor and to destabilise equal rights.[53] The globalisation and the linked increase of corporations led to an imbalance. Companies operating worldwide raised their power and influence and control a lot of the world's resources. The corporate power brought along rules favouring the global trade and weakening social objectives. This enhanced power requires an increase in corporate responsibilities. The mentioned differences in country's culture and laws and the strong influence of companies simply call for new corporate responsibilities and a closer look at the social welfare. The global economy reduced the power of single governments and their legitimate reach. Institutions as trade associations, non-governmental organisations and political cooperating systems occurred with the global business and try to fill the legislative gaps the globalisation brought along. As business formed a global economy, it has to be called to account. Business ethics and its instruments as code of ethics and Corporate Social Responsibility can be an excellent tool to fulfil these responsibilities.[54]

---

[52] Machan/Chester. 2002. A Primer on business ethics, pp. 157-177.

[53] DesJardins. 2009. An introduction to Business ethics, pp. 268-279.

[54] McIntosh/Waddock/Kell. 2004. Learning to talk, pp. 34-35.

III.1.7 Evidence in reference to customer power

The globalisation interconnected the world and brought along global corporations, who are selling worldwide and new communication tools, which are giving the consumers the opportunity to inform themselves better about the MNEs and their products and services. The increase in technology and the growing ecological consumer awareness respectively the increasing attention of consumers due to new communication technologies brought a change in business ethics. Ethical behaviour towards the consumers is considered as one of the important parts of business ethics. This fact is based on the circumstances that customer support is essential for business success and a damage of the corporate image due to unethical behaviour can stamp the buying habits of the consumer. Moreover, customer could start a rebellion and boycott corporations and their products. The globalisation made it even simpler for consumers to inform themselves about corporate ethical performance. Companies have to consider the basic consumer rights as product safety, moral marketing communication and fair treatment. They must also regard the increasing power of customers. The consumers oblige the market under circumstances of perfect competition. In reality, the consumer power decreases due to information asymmetries caused by the companies and the size of the market nowadays. Due to the restraint of full product information the business deal cannot be fair and the decreasing consumer sovereignty leads to an inefficient economic system. That creates ethical trouble. The outcome of this approach shows that the higher the consumer independence the more ethical is the business. This illustrates the influence of customers on corporate performance for one. Secondly, the consumers can use their consumption behaviour to control companies. The purchase manners can be used as 'votes' to support or boycott a specific product or company. With the increase in ethical consumption in the last decades and the better informed consumers, corporations really have to consider the new responsibilities. In the beginning of the new millennium, the first European wide survey about the social responsibilities of corporations, which included 12.000 consumers, was issued. This survey illustrated how important CSR is for the purchase decision as 70% of the European costumers said that the corporation's commitment to their social responsibilities is essential when buying. One in five Europeans is willing to pay more for environmentally and social products. Often consumers respond like this in studies, but their buying habits do not reflect these answers. The statement of 60% of the European consumers, which believe that businesses are not aware enough of their social responsibilities, illustrates that these consumers occupied themselves with this topic. More and more customers inform themselves about the ethical behaviour and business practices nowadays. This ethical consumption demonstrates the significance of customers in the regulation of business ethics. The strategically purchase behaviour cannot replace political action, but reflects the increase of corporations responsibilities and how consumer can express their moral believes and power through the multinational enterprises.[55] In the book 'values-driven business' the authors talk about their own practical experiences with social responsible enterprises. They also point out, the significance of customers due to the fact that there would be no business without them. They experienced that costumers become more faithful and due that are more willing to excuse errors, when they see the company's commitment. Consumers prefer corporations, which hold similar values and support the environment and the community and are willing to pay a higher price for the products. According to the authors, corporations which have strong relationships to their consumers have more potential and are more likely to stay in business during crisis. Social responsible corporations strengthen their business by working with their consumers and employees and integrate their interests into day-to-day business.[56] A survey of McKinsey in 2007 showed that environmental protection is positive in terms of image and profits. It also illustrated that the more corporations invest into social and environmental projects, the more they harm the environment. This behaviour is called 'green washing' and is used by companies to impress their consumers. 'Green washing' does not succeed over time as consumers are better informed these days and recognize this fraud. At this point, the corporate image can be even more damaged.[57] The strategically consumption increased in the last decades and has an impact on the corporate success. According to different surveys, 75-90 % of the consumers find corporations much more likable, when these are engaged in social and environmental activities. Moreover, 86% state that they would change their consumption behaviour to improve the world.[58]

III.1.8 Evidence by reference in to public media and NGOs

Business ethics became a prominent business topic, which cannot be neglected anymore. Multinational enterprises are facing way more challenges due to global business

---

[55] Crane/Matten. 2004. Business ethics: a European perspective, pp. 266-292.
[56] Cohen/Warwick. 2006. Values-driven business, pp. 9-23.
[57] Hartmann. 2009. Ende der Märchenstunde, pp. 10-22.
[58] ibid, pp. 147-152.

and need to consider business ethics to manage the ethical dilemmas. The media, consumers and various NGOs created a pressure towards firms and a demand of corporations looking for environmentally and ethically paths of doing their daily business. Managers' malpractices have a massive potential to harm the environment and the people involved due to an increasing power and influence of multinational enterprises. Companies started to realize the gain of ethical business practices and the positive influence on the firm of ethical behaviour.[59]

In the previous sections the need for business ethics was explained by philosophical and economical characteristics, the change as a result of globalisation and new consumer awareness. Besides, there are several other reasons, why it is important for corporations to deal with business ethics.

III.1.9 Critique on business ethics

Albert Carr argues that the interrelation between business and ethics is relative. In his essay "Is Business Bluffing Ethical?" he compares business with a game of poker. In his opinion business has its own moral rules and norms, as rules of a game, that differ from those of the society. Business as a separate activity is free from external moral understanding and though can act following its own standards and rules in its game. People tend to bluff in a poker game to reach their goal of winning and are not blamed as they play following the rules. According to Carr, business practices can also use the bluffing effect to maximize the profit and cannot be hold responsible for this as it happens according to the rules of the game. This theory of Carr cannot resist, as the environment of business, like the shareholders and consumers, are included in the game, if they wanted to or not. His statement of business as a game also does not withstand, due to the fact that business is a part of the economic fundament of our human existence and everything, even specialized fields, can be morally judged in this economy.[60]

Some authors discussed and still discuss the social and ethical responsibilities of corporations and managers and the question, if a corporation can be ethical. According to the canonical view, the maxim of businesses should be maximizing the profits for

---

[59] Crane/Matten. 2004. Business ethics: a European perspective, p. 12.

[60] Shaw. 1996. Business ethics, p. 15.

greater shareholder wealth by obeying the law. This train of thought does not include ethics and morality as the legislation is taking care of the rules and regulations.[61]

Milton Friedman is the most famous economist following the conviction that ethics and business are incompatible. He claims that the only social responsibility of a company is to increase the shareholders profits as they invest their money, which keeps the business alive. In Friedman's opinion, a corporation cannot have ethical responsibilities. Only humans, which have a moral understanding, can have responsibilities. Enterprises are legal persons, which can have legal responsibilities, but the company itself cannot have social responsibilities. According to the principal-agent-theory the corporation is owned by the principals, whose main goal is to increase their wealth. The manager, as the agent, has to fulfil this goal. The agent as a human person has a morality and can have ethical responsibilities, but he has to carry out the business in accordance to the owners perceptions. The manager can fulfil his social responsibilities in his private life, but not at the corporation's respectively the principals' expense. Friedman always stressed out that the main focus in business is to ask the question what the corporation implies for whom. In his means, a corporation has to maximize the shareholders returns, to offer products at a fair price to the customers and to pay an acceptable salary to the employees all in accordance with the law, which observes the ethical approach. The activities, which exceed the corporate responsibilities in sense of Friedman, are philanthropic. He judges that corporations can invest in social activities as long as these do not minimize the stockholders income, the employees' wages or increase the prices for the customer. In this train of thought, the only responsibilities of a manager are professional ones and these principles should guide him.[62]

The advocate Reilly and Kyj argued in the same manner as Friedman. They stressed out the incompatibility of ethics and business. Corporate Social Responsibility and any ethics are contradictory to the modern capitalism according to their view.[63]

Other authors also deny the need for business ethics as morally correct behaviour is a matter of course. If everybody would act according to their moral beliefs learned by parents or school, each person would act in an ethical manner and business practices as CSR would be unnecessary. The pure existence of laws does not mean that everybody is

---

[61] Adams/Maine. 1998. Business ethics for the 21st century, pp. 582.
[62] Friedman. 1970. The Social Responsibility of Business is to Increase its Profits.
[63] Thomson. 2001. Business Ethics as Corporate Governance, pp. 153-164.

observing them. Approaches, which try to restrict unethical behaviour can be useful, but the following of these ethical guidelines is not given and according the expectation of morality as a human law of nature, these approaches seem not be needed.[64]

III.1.10 Economical and reputational gain of business ethics

Some manager started to see the economical gain of CSR and being a good Corporate Citizen. Their main business goal to increase shareholders profit can be positively influenced by social and ethical behaviour. Leading a firm in an ethical manner can bring an improvement of consumer and employee satisfaction and reputation, a reduction of costs and competitive advantage.[65] The triple bottom line of businesses integrates not just financial, but also social and environmental aspects to reach a path of corporate growth and sustainable success. The social and environmental responsibilities can be included into the firm in a defensive or offensive way. Some corporations use CSR to defend themselves against damage claims or shareholders proposals connected with environmental or social topics, which could negatively distress the business. CSR is also used to protect the brand equity. Dealing with an ethical business approach in an offensive manner will reward the company positively. The offensive pattern of including CSR consists of developing goods, which are sustainable and environmentally friendly and consider social needs. This behaviour increases the consumer and employee satisfaction and leads to an overall improved reputation. A well-respected firm will attract talented and motivated employees and more opportunities of investments.

This social impact of a firm is reflected financially, not just by reducing costs from adversity, but also by enhancing competitive advantage. These are two of the major aspects of corporate social behaviour. The other two important factors of CSR symbolize the brand equity and the employee satisfaction and loyalty. The goodwill represents a company and its long-term success. In average are 40% of a firm's profits attributed to the reputation. If that is damaged due to unethical misbehaviour, the loss for the company is tremendous. The last aspect mentioned, covers the employees and their motivation to work at a specific firm. Surveys illustrated that corporations, which treat their employees in an ethical manner, face lesser strikes and law suits. Besides, it is less expensive and more extensive to recruit well-educated and motivated employees. Although, the financial return on investments in social and environmental activities

---

[64] Bernhardt. 2005. "Zum Nachholbedarf" in Unternehmensethik, p. 96.
[65] Martin. 2005. CSR and Public policy, pp. 78-79.

cannot be calculated that straightforwardly, the economical gain is proven. Many scientific studies showed a measureable impact on corporate proceeds. Furthermore, enterprises dealing with business ethics achieve better results in the long-term.[66] Unethical and amoral corporate behaviour can cause a lot of negative impacts. Firms can face a lot of legal risks and, as mentioned in the previous chapter, also consumer boycotts. Besides, they can face a loss of the company's name or even the marketplace. Companies, who implement and live ethical business practices, are more likely to have a stable organisation. Deloitte, a firm providing auditing services, demonstrated the increasing importance of business ethics by interviewing 5000 executives of the world's top public traded corporations in 2003. 98% of these managers considered ethical and social programs as an essential part of their organisation.[67]

III.1.11 Measurement of the impact of business ethics

In the last decades several measurement tools and voluntary benchmarks were created to assess the social and ethical performance of corporations. The Corporate Responsibility Index (CRI) was one of the first voluntary indicators of reference to compare social responsible business practices. The CRI measures different characteristics of the CSR performance and the relative significance and usefulness. Companies, which are member of this index, are scored by means of the evaluation of their CSR activities.[68]

A good preparation for successful business ethics is a well-working Corporate Governance and financial transparency. Investors discovered the advantages of social responsible companies and social investment funds were created as the Domini 400 Social Index, the FTSE4good or the Dow Sustainability Index. The Socially Responsible Investing (SRI) index includes only corporations, which successfully deal with social and environmental issues and fulfil the request of being ethical. Although some tobacco companies, for example, demonstrate social business behaviour and included CSR in their corporations, their products are regarded as unhealthy and they were not included in the SRI indices. Due to that fact, social responsible firms can be compared to companies, which are not appearing in these indices by means of their investment returns. All existing social responsible funds performed better than non-SRI indices in the last years. The Dow Sustainability Index increased 55% higher than the Dow Jones

---

[66] Roselle. 2005. The triple bottom line: building shareholder value, pp. 113-126.

[67] DesJardins. 2009. An introduction to Business ethics, p. 4.

[68] Jones/Pollitt/Bek. 2007. Multinationals in their communities, pp. 78-80.

Global Index since 1993. Studies illustrate that companies including CSR into their business practices improve their shareholder profit. Add to this, the overall results are better due to lower risks from social and environmental problems.[69]

III.1.12 Conclusion of hypothesis I

The questions asked in the beginning of chapter III can be answered with a methodological thought. A lack of morality due to a change in the society and many grey zones offered by the growing global economy lead to scandals and unethical behaviour of managers as illustrated in the media. The modern capitalism brought challenges along, which were too complex to face them with traditional methods. The challenges due to the globalisation could not be solved by national governmental action. As Aristotle claimed, the economical activities soil the humans' morality. To deal with this loss, Kant argued that everybody should treat his opposite as he wants to be treated. That coincides with the thought of consideration of public welfare. The idea of everybody is acting moral excludes the need for business ethics, but does not resist business dilemma situations and opportunistic behaviour of the agents.

The size of the global economy and the increased complexity of corporations caused problems, even dilemmas and grey zones in the distribution of social and ethical responsibilities. The unsuccessful established social ethics combined with various other problems in the governance leaves room for not observed gaps. Business ethics and its instruments can help to fill these gaps by moving the relationships between the government and its legislative and business and its increasing power in the globalised world. Business ethics is a strongly discussed topic and brought along some controversies. Albert Carr claims that business has its own moral; Milton Friedman even argued that business cannot have any social responsibilities and some authors say that business ethics is an oxymoron.[70]

Nevertheless, the gain of ethical business practices is conspicuous. As mentioned in this chapter, the impact of business ethics is not just by its financial nature, but also dependent on consumer power. A survey showed that customers form their image of a firm by its brand reflection, its financial results, but more than that by its business ethics

---

[69] Roselle. 2005. The triple bottom line: building shareholder value, pp. 117-121.
[70] Crane/Matten. 2004. Business ethics: a European perspective, pp. 7-19.

practices. The implementation of ethics deep down in the corporate soul, will bring better results, a stronger organisation and a better reputation.[71]

Business ethics and its instruments as compliance programs, social and sustainable business practices that keep in mind the community, environment and sustainability and codes of ethics are needed in today's multicultural global economy.

This evidence leads to the next hypothesis. In the second hypothesis, the impact of codes of ethics will be discussed under the condition that there is a need for ethics in business. Codes of ethics are used as a basis of corporate social behaviour and a guideline for all involved.

III.2 Hypothesis II: The efficient usage of codes of ethics can improve Corporate Governance

The previous parts of this paper illustrated the increasing importance of ethics and moral in the business context. Ethical cultures in organisations do not just appear. Corporations need to put effort in creating and implementing a corporate culture based on ethical understanding and behaviour. Codes of ethics form in this case the corner-stones of every ethics-based organisational culture. Especially in the global context, the meaning of codes is increasing. Corporations operating on a global level are facing in some areas gaps in governmental regulation. Codes of ethics represent a connection between the changes based on globalisation and corporate made legislative.[72]

But do these codes, which are created by corporations and institutions, really change the business behaviour? As codes are mostly voluntary, they do not represent binding law and even in the opposite case, their efficiency is not given. Although the law is legally binding, it is not guaranteed that everybody is following the legislative regulations.[73]

Why should codes of ethics be observed and why should they transform unethical business behaviour in ethical corporate performance? To answer questions like that, the phenomena of codes of ethics will be defined and reasons for their existence will be given in the next passage. Moreover, the importance of the right implementation of codes will be shown as the foundation for an effective and successful code.

---

[71] Milward-Oliver. 2005. The soul of the corporation, pp. 71-74.

[72] Crane/Matten. 2004. Business ethics: a European perspective, pp. 443-444.

[73] Koch. 2008. Wirtschaftsethik.

III.2.1 Definition and development of codes of ethics

Philosophers realized thousands of years ago that the human beings are in the position to influence their own conduct by the given freedom of choice. Moreover, people have a moral understanding and can distinguish between 'good' and 'bad'. Due to this freedom of choice and the differences in ethical understanding, humans need guiding principles to become aware of ethical actions especially in moral dilemmas. As Aristotle already said, humans need standards, which are based on moral existence and guide them through the fine line of 'good' and 'bad'. This principles and standards are replaced in the business world by codes of ethics.[74]

The OECD defines codes as 'commitments voluntary made by companies, associations or other entities, which put forward standards and principles for the conduct of business activities in the marketplace.' The codes are mainly voluntary, except from the legally binding codes required by the SOA, and therefore differ from legal regulations. That corporations volunteer to create such codes is dubious due to the fact that some codes were invented because of outside pressure from stakeholders, governments, media focus or trade unions. Nevertheless, codes of ethics can have legal significance and consequences. Corporate ethical statements represent a flexible complement towards the legislation and can help to decrease legal risk. As companies have different goals the intentions behind codes of ethics may differ too. These voluntary statements vary in their structure and content and take various names as codes of conduct, mission statements, codes of ethics or ethical guidelines. The three mostly covered topics inside these standards are human and labour rights and protection of the environment and are mainly directed at the same stakeholders, as there are the customers, shareholders, business partners, employees and governments.[75] In the mid-1990s about 95 percent of the Fortune 500 companies had already a code of ethics. Most of these firms, namely 90 percent, stated that they adopted their code in context with their corporate compliance system. The voluntary act of social accountability by companies is mainly in existence in Europe. At least 55 percent of European companies adopted their code in compliance with their stakeholders based on the belief that corporations have ethical and social responsibilities. In Canada and the United States, companies developed their ethical

---

[74] Machan/Chester. 2002. A Primer on business ethics, pp. xiii-xv.

[75] Lundblad. 2005. Some legal dimensions of corporate codes of conduct, pp. 386-391.

guidelines mainly due to other reasons.[76] The adoption of codes is not always based on such social initiatives, but is inspired in most of the cases by the idea of guiding employees and agents in the ethically right manner. Codes of ethics are the written basis of a firm's value system and moral ground rules. The ethical principles offer guidance for the people involved and show due its standards the ethically right way of behaviour.[77] As early as 1924, codes of ethics were mentioned in business journals as instruments, which cannot change moral positions in a magically manner. But they can be very effective and can lead to more respect and truth in business practices and relations.[78]

III.2.2 Various types of codes of ethics

In the development of codes of ethics and moral guidelines various institutions and businesses invented and adopted codes and therefore there exist many different forms of codes and several establishers. The literature is deviating from the actual number of different types of codes, but mainly codes are developed either by the company itself, trade associations, multi-stakeholder approaches or intergovernmental entities. The United Nations is making a difference between intergovernmental codes, so that they count five types of codes. The clustering of intergovernmental codes into model codes and international ones does not influence their same intention to guide businesses in their operations facing labour and human rights and environmental protection. These intergovernmental codes include for example the United Nations Global Compact, the OECD's Guidelines for Multinational Enterprises, the Global Sullivan Principles and the ILO's Tripartite Declaration of Principles Concerning Multinational Enterprises and Social Policy. These standards have no binding effect for MNEs, but represent a useful tool for companies. Multi-stakeholder codes are often addressing more people and are more effectively, due to the fact that these codes are adopted through a process of negotiations along with a variety of stakeholders and therefore cover more issues. The Social Accountability International is such a multi-stakeholder initiative. Codes, which mainly deal with industrial specific issues, are trade association codes. These cover specifically concerns of a particular branch and can be therefore very effective in a specific sector. The biggest share of codes represents the company codes. These

---

[76] Luo. 2007. Global dimensions of corporate governance, pp. 144-154.

[77] Schwartz. 2004. Effective corporate codes of ethics: perceptions of code users, pp. 323-324.

[78] Helin/Sandström. 2007. An inquiry into the study of corporate codes of ethics, pp. 253-254.

standards are commonly related to the corporation's mission and operations. Since the last decade, the relations to the suppliers and other business partners are more involved in corporate codes. Those voluntary codes vary extensively by enterprise because companies have different goals and resources. Surveys showed that corporations with closer relations to customers and well-known brands are more likely to adopt a corporate code.[79] A study of the OECD at the beginning of the twentieth century illustrates this division of different types of codes. According to the study, 48 percent of the codes are corporate initiatives, 37 percent are issued by industry sectors and trade associations, 13 percent by trade unions and two percent cover intergovernmental approaches.[80]

III.2.3 Motives for the implementation of codes of ethics

Multinational enterprises face a lot of challenges in global business and therefore have the most reasons to deal with codes of ethics. The global supply chain opened some gaps and grey zones, which are impeding for a healthy social welfare and environment. Corporations that face global competition fall back on unethical and misleading conduct to stay in the game of business.[81] Codes of ethics became a relevant instrument for setting standards, which promote social welfare and sustainability in business practices. These standards can help to create a fair global economic system.[82] Critics argue that codes are adopted by corporations as a reaction to the scandals, which occurred mainly in big firms in the last decades. The sceptics are of the opinion that the codes were just created due to external pressure after the misconduct in American companies. That is partly true. Since 2002 American firms have to implement codes of ethics according to the Sarbanes-Oxley-Act. Besides, corporations that want to be listed at the New York Stock Exchange and the Nasdaq Stock Exchange have to adopt and disclose such a code too. These reasons are not voluntary and can raise some scepticism. However, there are several other reasons for dealing with codes of ethics. Some corporations use them to protect their brand image and overall reputation or to enhance public relations. Codes of ethics are often invented to protect the firm's employees and to establish a behavioural

---

[79] Rudolph. 2005. The history, variations, impact and future of self-regulation, pp. 369-375.

[80] Shestack. 2005. CSR in a changing corporate world, pp. 106-107.

[81] Bass/Melchers. 2004. Die Diskussion um neue Instrumente zur sozialen und ökologischen Gestaltung der Globalisierung im Überblick, p. 6.

[82] Köpke/Röhr. 2003. Codes of conduct, pp. 48-50.

guideline for the employees. Besides, codes can help to improve the bottom line and are a basis to become a good Corporate Citizen.[83]

Codes of ethics are, as a part of Corporate Governance, also a very important factor of successfully governed corporations and help to keep international competitiveness. Codes are a basis of behavioural recommendations and assist to minimize the misconduct of employees and managers. In an era of easy accessible communication and information technology and a worldwide media network, such misconducts can lead to a damaged worldwide reputation.[84] Codes illustrate corporation's expectations about ethical and legal behaviour and support the detection of illegal practices. These ethical guidelines improve the awareness of unethical behaviour and corporate illegalities and help to avoid business corruption.[85]

As mentioned before, there are a wide range of codes existing nowadays and just as much reasons, why an organisation is adopting a code. Research showed that most of the codes have some overlaps in their main goals. The central aims behind codes are, besides their economical intends, protecting the environment, a reduction of worldwide poverty, elimination of child labour, an increase in human and labour rights, more equality between the genders and an improvement of the development of less developed countries.

The above named reasons are various and are very different in their nature. It does not matter, what exact reasons stands behind a code of ethics, more importantly is the right implementation into the organisation. The simple adoption of a code is neither an assurance of an effective code nor a promise for a good working ethical culture inside the company.[86]

III.2.4 Implementation and effectiveness of codes of ethics

The requirement of the effectiveness of codes of ethics is the right implementation into a healthy well-working ethical culture of an organisation. The importance of codes of ethics as a business ethics instrument and their influence can just be illustrated when the code is not adopted for 'window-dressing' but for real social means. Moreover, the

---

[83] Schwartz. 2004. Effective corporate codes of ethics: perceptions of code users, pp. 323-343.

[84] Lundblad. 2005. Some legal dimensions of corporate codes of conduct, p. 385.

[85] Luo. 2007. Global dimensions of corporate governance, p. 123.

[86] Shestack. 2005. CSR in a changing corporate world, p. 107.

effectiveness of such codes can just be proven when the ethical standards are right implemented and lived in an ethical culture. These conditions and the importance of codes in a globalised business world will be shown in the next sections.

Studies have exposed that unethical behaviour also occurs in organisations that have code of ethics. As the scandal of Enron showed, the existence of a code does not prevent from unethical behaviour of employees and managers. Due to insufficient ethics programs and ineffective ethical cultures of corporations a gap is originated between the code itself and its practical conversion. This gap mainly occurs because of poor designed codes and standards, which just set out rules that have to be followed and do not create a value based culture. Codes are in general also ineffective, when they are developed for the wrong reasons. Codes, which are adopted for marketing reasons or for legal risk reduction, cannot become a part of the corporate culture. A successful path of creating an effective code of ethics is the involvement of all stakeholders and most importantly the employees. During the whole development of a code employees should be asked about their daily challenges and their experiences with ethical dilemmas. Through this participation standards will be created, which will be taken seriously by employees and will change behaviour. Besides, the communication of this ethical guideline is of importance and needs to start at the top management. Manager can serve as a role model by communicating and living the standards of a code.[87] All these misconducts can be solved and the gap between the mere written code and its practical use can be closed by a healthy corporate culture. As every society needs its culture, organisations need the existence of shared norms and values too. A culture lived inside the firm guides to a strong organisation and leads to a positive attitude towards the firm by employees and managers. The strong commitment of the involved people and the ethical climate create an accepted value system and less failure and misconducts.[88] The ethical culture of a company is based on its mission. After establishing the mission statement, the corporate code can be developed and communicated. An important factor for an effective code is also the opportunity for employees and managers to declare unethical behaviour inside the company. An ombudsman or an ethical officer should be employed to secure the right dealing with the code and to take care of unethical or even illegal behaviour. 'Whistle-blowing' by the use of anonym ethical hotlines is a useful

---

[87] Webley/Werner. 2008. Corporate codes of ethics: necessary but not sufficient, pp. 405-415.

[88] Ferrell. 2005. A framework for understanding organizational ethics, p. 11.

instrument to expose unethical activities.[89] The content and language of the code and its ongoing administration is another crucial factor for a successful implementation. The content should include the responsibilities of employees and managers, inside information, possible conflicts, control of resources and assets, book keeping, bribery, antitrust laws, sexual harassment, political performance, environmental protection and employee rights, to name a few.[90] The language is essential for the commitment and efficiency. A hard language with fully-defined standards and in consideration of translation concerns as dialects leads to a clear communication of the meaning of a code for business partners and employees.[91] Besides, the regularly administration of the code and its instruments is central. The content of the code needs to be updated and the compliance to be monitored. Surveys inside the company can help to identify discrepancies in the code's existence. Moreover, the ethical standards are best implemented by using regular trainings for all participants.[92] A code should be more than a legalistic paper. The idea of an effective code should be developing a guideline that is living and actually used. That is best achieved by involving numerous stakeholders in the process of code creation and implementation.[93] The last, but no less crucial step is the auditing and monitoring of the code and the commitment towards penalties and sanctions by misconduct. Although, many companies adopted a code, there are few firms monitoring their ethical statements. Nevertheless, this part of the code implementation is essential for a well-working code. Corporations can monitor internally or by the use of learning models or consultation businesses.[94] According to the originators of the UN Global Compact the examination of a code by an external body should be a requirement. Due to the external control codes are more often observed and improved.[95] Studies illustrated that codes, developed due to social ideas and perfectly implemented, can strengthen the ethical culture of a corporation and lead to more ethical behaviour.[96]

---

[89] DesJardins. 2009. An introduction to Business ethics, pp. 83-85.

[90] Moore/Dittenhofer. 1992. How to develop a code of conduct, pp. 31-34.

[91] Mamic. 2004. Implementing codes of conduct, pp. 40-43.

[92] Moore/Dittenhofer. 1992. How to develop a code of conduct, pp. 35-36.

[93] Gilley/Robertson/Mazur. 2010. The bottom-line benefits of ethics code commitment, pp. 31-37.

[94] International Labour Office. 2001. Codes of conduct and multinational enterprises, chapter XII.

[95] Fussler/Cramer/Vegt. 2004. Raising the bar, p. 184.

[96] Cleek/Leonard. 1998. Can corporate codes of ethics influence behaviour?, pp. 622-624.

III.2.5 Benefits of codes of ethics

Codes of ethics can offer various advantages and economical gain for corporations as the requirements of the effective code, as declared before, are fulfilled. Interesting studies from the 1980s and 1990s proofed this fact. Surveys, published in the 1980s, discovered that codes of ethics do not influence the moral behaviour of people. The studies claim that codes are ineffective and not useful for corporations. That finding is connected with the wrong implementation of the codes. In the 1980s, the first corporate scandals occurred and companies started to adopt codes for 'window-dressing'. These written documents did not change anything in the corporate ethical culture as they were not lived. A questionnaire taken in the Fortune 500 companies illustrated that employees and managers in one-fifth of these firms did not know to whom the codes are addressed. Additionally, they had problems in reading and understanding the content of codes. Studies prepared in the end of the 80s and beginning of the 90s showed different results. Managers realized that the implementation of the code is an essential factor and changes the outcome of the ethical guidelines. Codes of ethics came of well in surveys and their efficiency and effectiveness in connection with social responsibility and ethical culture were realized. At this time, the first literature dealing with codes implementation and ethical culture improvement was published.[97] In the mid-90s the Ethics Resource Centre found a positive relation between moral behaviour and ethical codes in corporations, which have a living ethics program.[98] Besides, the sheer existence of formal code can change behaviour as results of employee interviews illustrate. According to the answers, the code also represents a symbolic function and reduces unethical and illegal behaviour. Employees are influenced by the presence of a code and have a higher commitment towards the company. In accordance with this questionnaire, the mere existence of a code creates a gain, respectively a decrease in violations and economical disadvantages resulting from unethical behaviour.[99] The economical and social gains, caused by effective codes, are therefore even better. Most of unethical corporate behaviour occurs due to short-term profit goals. However, the long-term success of a company is more essential and can create better stakeholder relations and competitive advantage. A well-working ethical culture, one of the most essential requirements for an effective code, strengthens the corporation's relationships. Ethi-

---

[97] Ibid, pp. 619-628.

[98] Webley/Werner. 2008. Corporate codes of ethics: necessary but not sufficient, p. 407.

[99] Helin/Sandström. 2007. An inquiry into the study of corporate codes of ethics, pp. 258-261.

cally-treated customers, employees and suppliers are more loyal and have a stronger commitment to the company and its interests. Customers and also investors are more likely to purchase from and invest in enterprises that they trust. Surveys showed that the development of an ethical culture and the adoption of a code can be costly, but the benefits are superior. An evidence of these advantages can be recognized by examine corporations that implemented ethical guidelines. Managers of such companies confirm the long-term improvement of ethical investments in the organisation.[100] Codes of ethics do not only increase the company's internal position, but also the social welfare. The corporate ethical statements help correcting the market failures, filling policy gaps and strengthen the social and moral standards in the society. Effective corporate codes, maintained by governments, NGOs and other institutions, can raise the overall social benefits.

The combination of ethical and business interests can achieve the best outcome economically, socially, environmentally and ethically.[101] An international survey of Corporate Responsibility, issued in 2008 by KPMG, a firm providing audit and advisory services, illustrates several gains for corporations following ethical guidelines. The study covers various firms, including the global Fortune 250 and the 100 largest companies by revenue. The examination shows that companies can better manage their risks by reflecting stakeholders' interests and understanding not only economic, but also environmental and social aspects. Besides, the survey shows the importance of ethical guidelines in context with corruption prevention. As corruption undermines free competition, it harms the long-term success of businesses. By adopting codes covering all kinds of bribery and extortion and disclosing these, corrupt business practices can be minimized. Another risk can occur in the supply chain. Firms are more responsible nowadays for unethical performance of their suppliers. By integrating the business partners into the ethical code and sharing the same moral beliefs, the risks in the supply chain can be reduced. The survey points out that companies, which link Corporate Responsibility and Corporate Governance, according to that combine their ethical code with their daily business practices and relations, are the leaders in their field.[102] The examination of corporations following the UN Global Compact reflects the linkage of better corporate performance with sustainable and social strategies. Most of these companies create projects with their stakeholders, have environmental targets as greenhouse gas reduction or invest in their employees' skills and satisfaction. Following the United Nations ethical code generates more value for the participating enterprises

---

[100] Gilley/Robertson/Mazur. 2010. The bottom-line benefits of ethics code commitment, pp. 31-37.

[101] Thomsen. 2001. Business ethics as Corporate Governance, pp. 154-160.

[102] KPMG international survey of Corporate Responsibility reporting 2008, pp. 46-50.

and competitive advantage. In the long run the quality of earnings is more important for these companies as the mere profit maximization.[103]

III.2.6 Critique on codes of ethics

Codes of ethics have logically critics as the whole phenomenon of ethics in business has. Some sceptics argue that codes are tools, which convert the legislative and the politics a private issue.[104] Codes' contents represent a mixture of moral regulations and limitations, which are created to promote the economic interests by appearing at the same time socially and ethically responsible. Besides, codes do not have the effect to influence or even change a person's moral attitude and commitment. Moreover, the critics dispute that the content of some codes is very vague and general or very detailed and not usable.[105] This condition of codes of ethics prevent from the right implementation, which is the main requirement of a code's effectiveness, as described before. And even if the code is really implemented, sceptics argue, the consideration is not guaranteed as there is no external auditing and verification systems in most of the cases.[106] Other authors are of the opinion that codes are not necessary because of good Corporate Governance, legal restrictions and internal auditing. This contradiction illustrates that some cynicism and resistance seems reasonable, but some scepticism of codes of ethics as purely 'window-dressing" are unfounded.[107]

III.2.7 Future outlook for codes of ethics

The future of the global economy needs a new claim and a different sight of managing business and politics due to the changes and challenges produced by the rushing world with its restless humans. The modern capitalism and the globalisation require new patterns. Corporate Governance and its influence will increase and help to govern the ethical challenges, which occur in business relations. Corporate Responsibility will become a substantial topic, which will concern everybody in the future.[108] The increasing pressure by consumers and the media will promote the multilateral ideas dealing with ethical, social and environmental objectives. The adoption of codes by multina-

---

[103] Fussler/Cramer/Vegt. 2004. Raising the bar, pp. 223-225.

[104] Köpke/Röhr. 2003. Codes of conduct, pp. 10-12.

[105] Shaw. 1996. Business ethics, pp. 9-10.

[106] McIntosh/Waddock/Kell. 2004. Learning to talk, p. 102.

[107] Schwartz. 2004. Effective corporate codes of ethics: perceptions of code users, pp. 323-343.

[108] McAlister/Ferrell. 2005. Corporate Governance and ethical leadership., p. 79.

tional enterprises brought many improvements in global human rights and labour rights and tightened up the focus on corporate activities created to improve social and environmental welfare. The discussion about corporate responsibilities and their regulative instrument of guiding codes have to continue.[109]

III.2.8 Conclusion for hypothesis II

This section illustrated the development of codes and the existing types of ethical guidelines. The adoption of codes seems necessary by closer analysis of the named reasons. But, as mentioned before, the mere development of a code is not the decisive factor. The right implementation and creation of an ethical culture leads to an effective code, which can be examined on its efficiency and gain. As the surveys illustrated there are plenty of advantages of codes of ethics and social and economical gains resulting from ethical guidelines. Although there is critique the positive effects for the governance of an enterprise predominate. Codes of ethics became state of the art in the last decades and their influence will increase. Corporations that made the code and its guidelines part of the business policy and daily operations enhanced competitiveness. The studies made it obvious that the implementation of clear standards and a social and ethical approach of business bring along advantages for a company. Codes of ethics represent a foundation on that an organisation is built and a background for moral understanding and business activities that are not covered by law. Nevertheless, there is still uncertainty around codes effectiveness and much more work needs to be done to increase the systems of implementation and monitoring in a general context to create comparability and more efficiency on a global basis.

---

[109] Rudolph. 2005. The history, variations, impact and future of self-regulation, pp. 383-384.

IV. Conclusion

The morally positive defined terms responsibility and sustainability have gained a lot of reputation and attention in the last decades. The society tends to demand more responsibility whenever conventional methods turn out negatively and to assign the guilt to the government or the economy. Especially corporations were blamed for inadmissible activities nowadays and business ethics is used here as a repairing principle. Nevertheless, moral and social behaviour should be a foundation of everybody. In the German constitution for example, it is written under article 14 paragraphs 2 that property obliged the owner and that the use should serve at the same time the owner and the general public welfare. This idea of corporate welfare behaviour serves the thought of business ethics. Ethical and social activities do not have to be non-profit and idealistic. Corporations can profit by operating their business with an implemented CSR program.[110]

The need for ethics in business seems reasonable in connection to the historical examination of business ethics as a part of the applied ethics and the inception of modern capitalism. The assumption of business as an adequate profession in accordance with the categorical imperative did not meet and points out the need for more moral in today's business. Moreover, the theory of Adam Smith and the increasing wealth for everybody guided by the 'invisible hand' left to much gaps for unethical behaviour. Opportunistically behaviour, caused by the division of ownership and control and the increase of responsibilities in growing corporations, created more unreasonable and unethical behaviour. The globalisation brought along more grey zones due to the differences in national cultures and legislatives. The recent scandals show that managers are willing to take advantage of these grey zones on a global context. That makes clear that there is a need for a new ethical relativism to take the various values and challenges into consideration. Through a greater than ever worldwide connection caused by new communication technologies the awareness of consumer and media increased and the influence of stakeholders became an important factor for enterprises. The new attention for business ethics is also the origin of discrepancy due to different perceptions of corporate responsibilities. Nevertheless, the gain is not measurable as the returns of other investments the economical and social advantages are tremendous. Enterprises, dealing with ethical prospects, have more loyal customers and employees, a better

---

[110] Hartmann. 2009. Ende der Märchenstunde, pp. 150-154.

reputation, competitive advantage, less consumer boycotts and score higher in Social Responsible Investing indices. The need for business ethics and the proved benefits are the basis for the examination of a specific part of business ethics, namely codes of ethics. These ethical guidelines cover the social responsibilities of companies, which are aware of the fact that they are a part of the public welfare and that there exist moral dilemmas that are not covered by any law. The global economy led to a shift in the relations between governmental legislative and business regulation. The implementation of codes of ethics as a part of the company's vision and operations can impact the Corporate Governance in several ways. The pure existence of codes minimizes misconduct. To illustrate the importance and main impacts of a code, the effectiveness has to be given. An effective code results from the right implementation and the social means behind the code. The ethical guidelines can change the behaviour of employees and managers and serve as a security net for dilemmas in daily business practices. Besides, the codes strengthen the organisation and are a good tool for risk reduction. Multinational enterprises have nowadays much power and influence and started therefore to accept the growing responsibilities. Codes of ethics facilitate the handling of these new responsibilities. By implementing the statement also in the supply chain, corporations can bring ethical opportunities of business behaviour inside the global network. The right dealing with codes can bring innovation and change for corporations in an ever-changing world and can increase the overall social welfare. Codes of ethics will never eliminate all criminal energy, but criminal laws cannot do that either and the society is still observing them. A critical reflection of the ethical orientation and moral principles of corporations will cause controversies, but will positively impact the Corporate Governance and serve a healthier moral philosophy of life.

V. References

Literature

- Adams, David / Maine, Edward. 1998. Business ethics for the 21st century. California: Mayfield publishing company.
- Albach, Horst. 2005. Unternehmensethik: ein subjektiver Überblick. In: Albach, Horst. 2005. Unternehmensethik und Unternehmenspraxis. In: Zeitschrift für Betriebswirtschaft, Special issue 5/2005. Wiesbaden: Betriebswirtschaftlicher Verlag Dr. Th. Gabler.
- Arns, Stephanie. 2008. Tue Gutes und profitiere davon. In. Upgrade, Vol.: 03/08.
- Bass, Hans / Melchers, Steffen. 2004. Die Diskussion um neue Instrumente zur sozialen und ökologischen Gestaltung der Globalisierung im Überblick. In: Bass, Hans / Melchers, Steffen. 2004. Neue Instrumente zur sozialen und ökologischen Gestaltung der Globalisierung. Codes of conduct, Sozialklauseln, nachhaltige Investmentfonds. Münster: LIT Verlag.
- Beauchamp, Tom / Bowie, Norman. 2004. Ethical theory and business. New Jersey: Pearson Education Inc.
- Beisheim, M. / Dreher, S. / Walter, G. / Zangl, B. / Zürn, M.. 1999. Im Zeitalter der Globalisierung? Thesen und Daten zur gesellschaftlichen und politischen Denationalisierung. Baden-Baden: Nomos-Verlagsgesellschaft.
- Bernhardt, Wolfgang. 2005. "Zum Nachholbedarf" in Unternehmensethik. In: Albach, Horst. 2005. Unternehmensethik und Unternehmenspraxis. In: Zeitschrift für Betriebswirtschaft, Special issue 5/2005. Wiesbaden: Betriebswirtschaftlicher Verlag Dr. Th. Gabler.
- Böhm, Hans. 1979. Gesellschaftliche verantwortliche Unternehmensführung. Weilheim/Teck: Bräuer Verlag.
- Cleek, Margaret / Leonard, Sherry. 1998. Can corporate codes of ethics influence behaviour? In: Journal of Business Ethics, 17, 1998.
- Cohen, Ben / Warwick, Mal. 2006. Values-driven business. San Francisco: Berrett-Koehler Publishers.
- Crane, Andrew / Matten, Dirk. 2004. Business ethics: a European perspective. New York: Oxford University Press.

- DesJardins, Joseph. 2009. An introduction to Business ethics. New York: McGraw-Hill.
- Ferrell, O.C.. 2005. A framework for understanding organizational ethics. In: Peterson, Robert / Ferrell, O.C.. 2005. Business ethics. New challenges for business schools and corporate leaders. 2005. New York: M.E. Sharpe, Inc.
- Fussler, Claude / Cramer, Aron / Vegt, van der, Sebastian. 2004. Raising the bar, creating value with the United Nations Global Compact. UK: Greenleaf publishing.
- Friedman, Milton. 1970. The Social Responsibility of Business is to Increase its Profits. In: The New York Times Magazine, September 13, 1970.
- Gilley, Matthew / Robertson, Christopher / Mazur, Tim. 2010. The bottom-line benefits of ethics code commitment. In: Business Horizons, 53, 2010.
- Hartmann, Kathrin. 2009. Ende der Märchenstunde. Wie die Industrie die LOHAS und Lifestyle-Ökos vereinnahmt. München: Blessing-Verlag.
- Helin, Sven / Sandström, Johan. 2007. An inquiry into the study of corporate codes of ethics. In: Journal of Business Ethics, 75, 2007.
- International Labour Office. 2001. Codes of conduct and multinational enterprises. Geneva.
- Jones, Ian / Pollitt, Michael / Bek, David. 2007. Multinationals in their communities – a social capital approach to corporate citizenship projects. Hampshire: Palgrave MacMillan.
- Karmasin, Matthias / Litschka, Michael. 2008. Wirtschaftsethik – Theorien, Strategien, Trends. Berlin: Lit-Verlag.
- Köpke, Ronald / Röhr, Wolfgang. 2003. Codes of conduct – Verhaltensnormen für Unternehmen und ihre Überwachung. Köln: PapyRossa Verlag.
- Lundblad, Claes. 2005. Some legal dimensions of corporate codes of conduct. In: Mullerat, Ramon. 2005. CSR, the corporate governance of the 21st century. The Hague: Kluwer law international.
- Luo, Yadong. 2007. Global dimensions of corporate governance. US: Blackwell publishing.
- Machan, Tibor / Chester, James. 2002. A Primer on business ethics. Maryland: Rawman & Littlewood Publishers, Inc.
- Mamic, Ivanka. 2004. Implementing codes of conduct. How businesses manage social performance in global supply chains. Geneva: Greenleaf Publishing.

- Martin, Felix. 2005. CSR and Public policy. In: Mullerat, Ramon. 2005. CSR, the corporate governance of the 21st century. The Hague: Kluwer law international.
- McAlister, Debbie Thorne / Ferrell, O.C.. 2005. Corporate Governance and ethical leadership. In: Peterson, Robert / Ferrell, O.C.. 2005. Business ethics. New challenges for business schools and corporate leaders. 2005. New York: M.E. Sharpe, Inc.
- McIntosh, Malcolm / Waddock, Sandra / Kell, Georg. 2004. Learning to talk, Corporate Citizenship and the development of the UN Global Compact. Sheffield: Greenleaf Publishing.
- Milward-Oliver, Gerald. 2005. The soul of the corporation. In: Mullerat, Ramon. 2005. CSR, the corporate governance of the 21st century. The Hague: Kluwer law international.
- Moore, Wayne/Dittenhofer, Mortimer. 1992. How to develop a code of conduct. USA: The Institute of internal auditor research foundation.
- Mullerat, Ramon. 2005. The global responsibility of business. In: Mullerat, Ramon. 2005. CSR, the corporate governance of the 21st century. The Hague: Kluwer law international.
- Newton, Lisa. 2005. Business ethics and the natural environment. Oxford: Blackwell Publishing.
- Pfitzer, Norbert / Oser, Peter. 2003. Deutscher Corporate Governance Kodex: Ein Handbuch für Entscheidungsträger. Stuttgart: Schäffer-Poeschel Verlag.
- Richard, George T. De. 1989. There is ethics in business ethics; but there's more as well. In: Journal of business ethics, Vol. 8.
- Roselle, James. 2005. The triple bottom line: building shareholder value. In: Mullerat, Ramon. 2005. CSR, the corporate governance of the 21st century. The Hague: Kluwer law international.
- Rudolph, Phillip. 2005. The history, variations, impact and future of self-regulation. In: Mullerat, Ramon. 2005. CSR, the corporate governance of the 21st century. The Hague: Kluwer law international.
- Schmeisser / Rönsch / Zilch. 2009. Shareholder Value approach versus Social Responsibility. München: Rainer Hampp Verlag.
- Schwartz, Mark. 2004. Effective Corporate Codes of ethics: Perceptions of Code Users. Toronto. In: Journal of Business Ethics, Vol. 55.

- Senge, Peter / Smith, Bryan / Kruschwitz, Nina / Laur, Joe / Schley, Sara. 2010. The necessary revolution – how individuals and organizations are working together to create a sustainable world. London: Nicholas Breatley Publishing.
- Shaw, William. 1996. Business ethics. California: Wadsworth publishing company.
- Shestack, Jerome. 2005. CSR in a changing world. In: Mullerat, Ramon. 2005. CSR, the corporate governance of the 21st century. The Hague: Kluwer law international.
- Skousen, Mark. 2007. The big three in economics: Adam Smith, Karl Marx, and John Maynard Keynes. New York: M.E. Sharpe, Inc.
- Thomas, Rosamund. 2005. Business ethics. In: Mullerat, Ramon. 2005. CSR, the corporate governance of the 21st century. The Hague: Kluwer law international.
- Thomson, Steen. 2001. Business Ethics as Corporate Governance. In: European Journal of Law and Economics, Vol. 11, No. 2, 2001, The Netherlands.
- Walsh, Mark / Cowry, John. 2005. CSR and corporate governance. In: Mullerat, Ramon. 2005. CSR, the corporate governance of the 21st century. The Hague: Kluwer law international.
- Webley, Simon / Werner, Andrea. 2008. Corporate codes of ethics: necessary but not sufficient. In: Business Ethics: A European review, Vol. 17, Number 4, 2008.

Internet

- http://www.business-ethics.org/primer.asp. Retrieved on 22/05/2010.
- http://www.allbusiness.com/glossaries/business-ethics/4962856-1.html. Retrieved on 22/05/2010.
- Geißler, Cornelia. 2004. Was ist compliance management? URL: http://www.harvardbusinessmanager.de/heft/artikel/a-620695.html. Retrieved on 25/05/2010.
- Koch, Miriam. 2008. Wirtschaftethik:"Es ist naiv, nur mit guten Menschen zu rechnen". In: Die Presse.
  URL: http://diepresse.com/home/wirtschaft/economist/365168/index.do?from=suche.intern.portal. Retrieved on 20/06/2010.
- Spitzeck, Heiko. 2008. Moralische Organisationsentwicklung: Was lernen Unternehmen durch die Kritik von Nichtregierungsorganisationen? Basel. URL: http://www.dnwe.de/forum-we-2-2009-rezensionen.html#rez2. Retrieved on: 14/06/2010.